Serotonin

An anthology of poetry and prose on mental illness, suicide prevention, and neurodivergence edited by Sean W. Lynch

serotoninpress.com

First Edition, November 2024
Copyright © by Sean W. Lynch, Editor

Published in the U.S.A. by Serotonin Press, Philadelphia, PA. The authors retain all rights to their works. Cover art by Mackenzie Moore.

Table of Contents

Introduction

I started Serotonin as an online poetry journal in May of 2020 at the height of the Covid-19 pandemic after receiving my first unemployment check. It had been two months since I was laid off from work in the restaurant industry and like many others who lived alone in quarantine I struggled with my mental health. Ten years prior I was hospitalized for an attempted suicide and sought various treatments for major depression throughout my 20's. I realized that the Covid-19 pandemic exacerbated my mental illness, and turned (as I had before in other times of crisis) to writing poetry to help deal with it.

As I searched for literary publications to submit my work to, I felt that there needed to be a space that published literature that focused solely on mental illness, and so Serotonin began. I set aside a portion of my unemployment to pay contributors who wrote poetry and short prose about their mental illnesses. The project quickly became popular on social media and I received hundreds of submissions from people around the world. This anthology collects a selection of 115 works of poetry and prose originally published on what is now serotoninpress.com (formerly serotoninpoetry.org). Of the 115 writers published within, 34 are of international origin and 81 from the USA, with 12 from Nigeria, 6 UK, 5 Canada, 2 Singapore, and 1 writer each from Australia, Greece, India, Philippines, Ireland, Pakistan, Hong Kong, France, and Uganda.

From teenagers to ninety-year-olds, from Vancouver to Philadelphia, Nigeria to Uganda, first-time published writers to famous poets, Serotonin: an anthology on mental illness and suicide prevention shares poems and prose with an incredible amount of diversity. The diversity contained within not only lies in the range of ages, geography, ethnicity, religion, gender, and LGTBQ+ identities but also the neurodiversity of the contributors. This anthology is a collection of writings that reflect on the spectrums of what have been long referred to as "mental illnesses" as well as the more recent term neurodivergence. I am still using the problematic term of mental illness here for lack of more widely recognized words to describe the experiences of individuals who are not neurotypical.

I've organized this anthology into different sections in order to provide a framework for understanding these brilliant writers in the context of what they're experiencing. The different sections often overlap with one another. A poem may deal with multiple categories, i.e. ADHD and anxiety, but placed under whichever fits best overall. Each piece is written based on the experiences of the author. There is no speculative fiction/poetry involved. That being said, there are creative liberties taken, and no depictions in the following works are of anyone who has not shared them willingly, voluntarily, and with full consent.

I am concerned with the reader's experience in confronting these difficult topics. Instead of offering various trigger warnings at the beginning of each piece, please understand that this anthology on a whole deals with a variety of what may be considered disturbing subject matters. The way that the sections are sequenced should help in forewarning the reader of whether they want to continue in reading on the subject matter, with the intensity of the pieces generally increasing the further one reads a section.

There are ten sections to this anthology: Depression, Anxiety, ADHD, OCD, Schizophrenia, Autism, Bipolar Disorder, Eating Disorders, Trauma, and Self-Harm. Take particular care in recognizing the graphic nature of works under eating disorders, trauma, and self-harm. The trauma section features some works that deal with sexual assault. Both eating disorders and self-harm have depictions of bodily harm that some may find unsettling.

I am honored and excited to share these poems and prose with more readers by publishing this anthology. Serotonin went on hiatus for 2 years between 2022-2024, so this anthology is a long time coming. I want to thank all contributors, readers, and editors who have helped me out on the masthead over the years. A huge thank you to Mackenzie Moore for the lovely artwork. Thank you very much to Kavita Khajuria for her support and her work on book reviews for Serotonin. I would lastly like to acknowledge the contributors to Serotonin who have passed away, including Simon Perchik, Roberta Santlofer, and Michelle Fulkerson.

-Founding Editor, Sean W. Lynch

Below are some resources for suicide prevention (note that the national suicide prevention hotline may in extreme circumstances contact emergency authorities if they find you to be a threat to yourself or others. The other hotlines do not contact police):

National Suicide Prevention Hotline: 988 (Call or Text)

Samaritans NYC: 212-673-3000

Thrive Lifeline 313-662-8209 (Text Only)

Trans Lifeline: 877-565-8860 (For Trans Callers)

Call Blackline 1-800-604-5841 (For BIPOC Callers)

Depression

Poem by Simon Perchik

This is it –a match, wood, lit
the way a butterfly returns
by warming its wings wider
and wider, one against the other
then waits for the gust to spew out
as smoke lifting you to the surface
–this single match circling down
half on fire, half held close
is heating your grave, has roots
–embrace it, become a flower
fondle the ashes word by word
that erupt from your mouth
as an old love song, a breeze
worn away by hills and the light
coming back then lying down.

Good Morning by Heidi Seaborn

Maybe it's my birthday
or just the blinds blinking
into little sparklers. I have wishes
lined up like the champagne bottles
and cigarettes on the windowsill.

Last night, I rode a crazy pill to the moon—

& this morning, look in the mirror—
I'm flush, a mimosa tree all summer.

Well then, I think I'll eat toast
with apricot jam, powder my nose
with sugar, grind coffee into my brows,
brush nectarine on my cheeks.

Call it good, call it a day.

Windows by Ra Vandey

There is a window in the apartment
of the floor above me. Its decades-old
outline creates a picture frame
visible from my bed.
At night the lamp on the ancient nightstand
drags itself to life. It illuminates the sitting room
in dusty hues that remind me of small-town funeral parlors
and the clicking of old women's pearls.
I have never seen whoever resides in the home
that belongs to that window,
but I think about what kind of person they must be.
I wonder, sometimes, if I am like their apartment,
colored in with the stale decorations of existence
and nothing to prove I was there but lights on timers.
Is there someone still alive in here, or have I become
just a body in the sitting room?

Depression by Janet McCann

I think of my parents living through it,
spaghetti with home-grown tomatoes for dinner,
an egg for breakfast. Downturn, slump.
I feel it in my stomach, hollow, hole,
concavity, dent, lack of roundness,
off-kilter sphere. There are pills for it
of course, they smooth out the sharp shards
at the bottom of the dent, but the declivity
is still there. "Hard times," my grandfather
said. They lived mostly on the kitchen
garden. Preserves. I saw the jewels of their jars
shining on basement shelves. Slowdown. Standstill.
I have the megrims. There is a crater
in the macrocosm, nothing
is filling it up.

Dogs Save Lives by William Musgrove

Last night, I stayed up watching dog videos. In one, a Border collie swam out to the middle of a lake and rescued a drowning fawn. In another, a German shepherd detected a bomb inside an airport. In another, a Great Dane pulled his owner from a burning building. My dog isn't heroic.

She's just a normal dog, an Irish terrier named Mabel. Light peeks out from under the blinds. It's morning. Maybe it's early afternoon. I shift onto my side and pull my blanket over my head. I bring my knees to my chest. Mabel sniffs my perimeter. I lift the blanket, and she steps inside. She spins in a circle before plopping down next to me. I whine. Mabel whines in solidarity.

Minutes or hours pass. Mable crawls toward the edge of the bed. The blanket folds around her quadrupedal body until only her nose and eyes stick out, and she resembles a nun. She shoves her face into my face. She licks my cheeks. She's unrelenting.

"Okay, okay."

With the blanket draped over my shoulders, I shuffle to the kitchen. I fill her food and water bowls. Then I go lie on the couch.

Crunch, crunch. Lap, lap.

Mabel skips into the living room. She bites her leash and drags it off the coffee table. She drops the six-foot rope on a cushion. She nuzzles it toward me.

"No, not now."

I turn so I'm facing the back of the couch. Mabel barks. She barks again.

"Fine, fine."

I get dressed. I slip on my sneakers. I hook the leash to Mabel's collar. I open the front door. The sunlight's harsh. I shield my eyes, waiting for my pupils to adjust. Mabel tugs me forward, and I take my next steps of the day.

My Shrink's Waiting Room by Gary Bloom

Everyone's head stays down
studying the rudely stained carpet
(the Prozac tremors knocking the coffee from our cups)
afraid to look up and be assessed
except for the psychiatrists
who exit their paneled (padded?) offices
and glad hand new arrivals like Walmart greeters
then whisk them away.
They will sternly look you over
to see if you belong to them
or just to make you nervous.
The lady with the appointment before me
for the past four years
looks far beyond to some distant focal point
while I make my way to the vacant chair
where I sit uncomfortably
in someone else's warmth.

Resolve by Claire Taylor

I am trying to be more intentional. I hate when people use this word. Intentional. Present. Mindful. Take notice while washing the dishes, a mindfulness exercise suggests. Notice the suds, the gloss of the bubbles. Pay attention to the sound of the water, spilling from the tap, hitting the sink basin, gliding over your skin. Focus on how the water swirls down the drain. Notice how each day is a series of small, repetitive tasks stacked atop each other. Not enough to fill you up, to make you whole, but enough to weigh you down. Note how the weight settles into your lower back, aching in the center, a pain originating deep in the bone. Something structural. Something you are too old to bother correcting. Focus on your hands scrubbing the dishes. How the skin, grown loose with age, pools around your knuckles. Notice how you barely recognize these hands. Weak and sore, always struggling with jar lids. Notice how you barely recognize yourself. The folds of your middle like waves, one on top of the other. Note what it feels like to drown. Pay attention to the sound of your scream, echoing behind your eyes, muffled by your pillow, beating against you like a bat through the twilight sky as you stand at the sink. Notice the heat of the water. The way the food stains lift from the plates. Everything washing clean. Everything disappearing. Notice how the sun fades away. How the sky melts from orange to purple to impenetrable black. How night descends without a care. Take note of how another day is ending and here you are, still standing.

·

Tucked by Kara Knickerbocker

When I arrive home, my mother is already waiting at the door.

We walk toward the room I grew up in, each movement folded

into silence. She doesn't know how to ready depression,
lie down next to it. She only knows that a good cleaning

involves toughness, makes everything transparent. Like
always,

she still wants to make my bed. *Rest, you'll feel better* she
soothes,

as her hands smooth out fresh sheets, her arms billowing to
the sky

as if she was creating heaven. Here, my grief is the mattress &
now,

there is something holy about how my body collapses
onto it & she covers me, pure, like a prayer—

Before You Name the Blade by Oluwatomiwa Ajeigbe

Before you name the blade after your trauma, remember what your Physics teacher said when you were in high school. Before you name the blade after your depression, remember the law of conservation of energy: *can neither be created or destroyed but changed from one form to another.* Before you name the blade something so heavy your mother wouldn't be able to pronounce it, remember that you won't be ending the pain but transferring it, remember that you won't escape the void—you'll only let it burst out of you to swallow everything you left behind. Before you name the blade on the pulse at your wrist, remember that someone somewhere loves you.

Depression Insomnia by Sean Hanrahan

Depression insomnia caused my street to buckle
as if the external world was collapsing,
my internal world had already.
Part of me clung to a bombed-out skyscraper
tilted back in terror of the sky.
My former aspirations, two murder planes,
and a stupid one-sided love affair created
a new Manhattan of places to avoid.
Subway grates became portals
I wished I could sink through like a lesser demon.
I left the city for suburbia, traded purpose for sleeplessness.
My knees wobbled at the rapid descent to a new hallucinated
reality.
I became a hell-sent emissary, couch-ridden and irritable.
Now, the video store clerk knew me by name
as I counted out spare change to rent escape.
I thought my parents' practical brown carpeting was a dying
meadow
in Central Park where Shakespearean flowers once bloomed.
I had sunk to a substratum below even hell. I would close my
eyes until the world solidified.
My life crusted over like my unwashed hair.
I only felt grounded when I could smell that familiar
depressive stink and exhale.

Day in Bed by Roberta Santlofer

Decided to spend the day in bed.
Coffee works...some.
Medication? I don't know.
Today, did things housewives do.
Cloroxed out bathtub: Toxic experience.
Fed cat & fed cat!
Laundry.
How does one do old age?
Certainly I don't know.
I knew raising children &
Work. Avocations made
Sense during that period.
And now? Now! What?

The Day Bruce Springsteen Saved My Life by Francesca Moroney

On a Tuesday morning in the middle of January, I sob loudly inside my car, parked in the school lot. Frost covers the windows. Behind me, the baby sleeps in her car seat, head slung low on her chest. I am four months postpartum with my fourth child, and my body feels like lead, struggling even to turn the key in the ignition. Around me, busy parents enter their cars, alone, and I envy them—all of their children safe in the care of others. Cars exit the lot, turn signals blinking in the brittle light, but I can't move. It's not the crying that keeps me inert, but this pressure below my sternum, a lump that feels like a large, hungry animal flung against my chest, plus a feeling that everything I've ever loved is waving goodbye from behind a thick, soundproof pane of glass. There is nothing in my life that does not exhaust me. I do not know how I will get home. I fear I will petrify and my other children will find their sister at the end of the day covered in tears and urine, or that I have forgotten how to drive, how to yield at intersections and pull over for emergency vehicles. I know I must not stop atop the railroad tracks, but I worry I might ignore that knowledge when the time comes. I am still crying and the baby still sleeps when I hear Bruce Springsteen sing, *You've been hurt and you're all cried out.* Suddenly, I feel somehow less original—relieved by the presence of someone else's pain and depression inside my head. If the achy, angsty voice from within my speakers can make his own unbearableness sublime, surely it can make mine bearable. The lyric escapes my lips quietly, like a secret, or a prayer—after all, I am not so far gone as to have forgotten how vital it is to not wake a sleeping baby. My hands are cold on my hot cheeks when I wipe away my tears, and I hope I will remember to warm them before lifting my daughter from her seat and carrying her inside. I put the car into gear and check my blind spots before pulling away, trusting in Bruce when he promises *a thin white line* of love, alive at the edge of the dim highway, a beacon I might follow, a way to survive, at least, the drive home.

Weathered by Lisa Weber

Sometimes she thinks it won't stop raining. Like someone was preparing a bath and walked away. Someone exhausted, bones and soul aching from carrying so much grief. Maybe they went to lie down for just a moment and didn't have the strength to get back up. The faucet still on, the plug still in, and the water continues to flow. It spills over the tub and puddles on the bathroom floor. Waves crash into the hallway and water cascades down the staircase. The entire house becomes a sea of sadness.

Maybe someone comes home, worn out and wanting only to wash away the day. They open the door and release a tsunami, the water carrying whole lives out into the street and down into the darkness of the sewer drain. And maybe someone calls the insurance company to try to piece together the ruined lives. But the insurance company wants to haggle over the costs because loss doesn't mean the same thing to them. They see damage, but not the damaged.

Mold grows in the walls of the house. Black and poisonous. But not all of it is visible. Some of it hides in the dark corners of closets, in the basement, in the attic. The places where secrets are stored and memories haunt.

Someone thinks they need a new house. A clean, dry house where they can start all over. But they can't afford that. Anyway, they carry the mold inside them. They'll never be clean and dry.

Sometimes she thinks it won't stop raining.

Remember by Olly Nze

When you find yourself awake, again,
At two in the morning wondering when
your body began to mistake fistfuls
of diazepam for aspirin,
And you are sitting in rainwater wanting to call your
Boyfriend—a man, raised by men, raised by men—
Just to hear him scuff at your whimpers as you
Beg him to finally say he loves you,
Or you find yourself cold and alone, in
The small town you swore you would never
Return to, wondering what a two-storey
Fall will do to your spine,
Remember
You have been here before.

Remember
You will be here again.
You will die as many times as it takes you to live.
And if you only get to live once, it will be enough

Wanting Away by Jerry Chiemeke

You are lying on the floor, five inches away from the mattress. It's no cooler down on this rug, but you are not exactly in search of lower temperatures. Curled on the 6 × 4 and breathing slowly is probably all the warmth you need, possibly the one thing that matters now...but maybe you are not out for comfort in these moonless hours.

You want space to mull over, to stare your soul's emptiness in the eye, to brood over your disillusionment without the distraction of loving arms.

Surfing YouTube puts both your battery and your mobile data under pressure, and googling your favourite musician has long become an unexciting pastime. You don't entertain the thought of praying either; for one, you can't help but feel that it's an easy pathway to sleep, and in any case, you took a shot at that option hours ago, but you felt no better. You can't blame Him though, He's a pretty busy Being, deserving of some real slack, even when your tears soak the communion railings, even when your knees sink into the tiles.

It gets to you, looking spoilt for choice one moment and left with nothing the next. It gets to you, being overlooked again and again, no significant additions on the last Google search of your name. It gets to you, populating your blood stream with blue and yellow pills just to boost stubbornly deficient serotonin levels.

You wonder if the tight shutting of eyes and quick gulping of water is even of any use: the disco hall segment of your life ended with your early 20s and the sound of bluesy guitars make up the soundtrack for your hours now.

You're exhausted; of trying so hard to be funny in person to correct notions of you from people who couldn't be bothered, of having to explain why communication is a real chore for you, of making her see that when you say nothing it's not because you're getting drawn to someone else, of dealing with "why so melancholic?" inquiries and "I just wanted to check on you" platitudes.

You are done with trying to make yourself understood or likeable, and you have come to terms with the fact that nobody's going to love you right, that a hundred soothing text messages will never be enough, that God himself would have to come down if the pile of broken pieces that is yourself stands any chance of ever being put together.

You've run out of tickets to the pity party, and you just want to be away, this version of "away" being more of a feeling than a place, that fever pitch desire to swim across planets and watch your body float from the sidelines. Colourful photos from birthdays of acquaintances on your Instagram page are unable to cancel out the greyscale that is your default hue, and you know for sure that the ceasefire from the wars in your head has run its course.

Baptisand by Samuel A. Adeyemi

To drown the devil, the girl is lowered into a pool of water.

When she is pulled out, her hair quickly cascades—a pair of

waterfalls rolling down each shoulder. & as her eyes open,

she confesses to the priest; *Baba, I felt angels sanctify my soul.*

I begin to wonder the anomaly in my immersion. When the

water touched my body, I swear, it was just water. Even as

the oil drew a crucifix on my skin, no spectre was blazed by

the holy grease. I do not confess this lack. I stay silent as silk.

Yet all the clergy break into glee, my ears servile to a waste

of *hallelujah.* I want to say, it is not healing if nothing alters

in the plagued, that all the demons they think are dead only
sleep. Still, I resist vowelling my truth. I know that I am not

permeable to miracle, but I must keep on following the lie;

that I am void of the spirits persecuting my peace. Or is this

not what our elders preach? *Brethren, do not be deceived—*

depression is but a spirit of Satan. Why then will it surprise

me, that when I ask my people for therapy, I awaken before

the feet of an exorcist?

goooooood morning, america! by Maitreyi Parakh

the women on the radio are lying to us. i picture them sitting
in a recording studio somewhere in new york or los angeles
or chicago / bubble gum pink lips & long

sharp nails that could tear through the fragile skin of my
wrists. when the nurse in powder-blue scrubs comes back to
pull the blood or morphine out of my veins,

i hop off the stool and roll down my shirt sleeve. *thanks, but
not today, i think.* i remember this part, a 2012 summer
morning & i'm in love with the boy next door. his

teeth are biting into my wrists, and i'm letting him because i
love you sounds too much like goodbye / because there are
gunshots firing in the background & i don't

care enough to check whether he's dead yet. the woman on tv
is holding my heart in her left hand, reaching out to me with
her other one / *buy one, get another*

free! / what does it matter when every bit of kronos' soul
rests in this pill bottle? take your hands off my wrists, i say,
you can take me home when these broken records finally stop
playing.

Premenstrual Dysphoric Disorder by the Numbers by Lori Sebastianutti

One week of contentment, two weeks of misery, one week of recovery. Four letters. PMDD. One more than its gentler cousin, PMS. Eight defining characteristics: depression, irritability, difficulty concentrating, lack of interest in activities once enjoyed, moodiness, increased appetite, extreme fatigue, feeling out of control. Twelve, the number of days per cycle you experience said symptoms. Forty-four, the age at which you were diagnosed. Three years of experiencing symptoms before an official acknowledgment. Two, the number of psychiatrists it took to diagnose you. 2013, the year PMDD was added to the list of depressive disorders in the *Diagnostic and Statistical Manual of Mental Disorders* (*DSM-5*). One mental disorder it's often confused with: Bipolar Disorder. One main hormone that is to blame: Progesterone. Four different treatment options: oral contraceptives, antidepressants, chemically-induced menopause, hysterectomy. Three, the number of antidepressants it took to find the right fit. Two brain chemicals your medication targets: Serotonin and Norepinephrine. One, the number of sleeves of Golden Oreo cookies you can consume in one sitting two or three days before your period arrives. Two children who have to hear you say "sorry, mommy can't play Monopoly right now because she has to lie down." One, the number of CBT (Cognitive Behavioural Therapy) courses for anxiety you took after you were diagnosed. Zero, the number of people you knew had PMDD before your diagnosis. One person, you suspect had the condition—your mother, an Italian-immigrant, stay-at-home mom who would never give credence to a mood disorder but who would simply "push through" because caring for your six children is more important than taking care of yourself. Five, the approximate percentage of people worldwide who have PMDD. Fifteen percent of people with this disorder will attempt suicide in their lifetime. Six, the number of years left before you go into menopause according to national statistics when you may see some relief. Zero, the number of known cures. The number of times a sufferer will encounter misogyny while seeking support: countless.

Mashed by Helen Bowie

Sprawled across the sofa, reaching for the remote
Side effects may include nausea, fatigue, loss of appetite
SSRIs may take two weeks, there is no instant gratification
To be found at the bottom of a bag of potato smileys
Potato frownies – for when you don't want to grow up
but also you aren't happy.

The oven timer rings out
Like a round of applause
For doing the self care of
Eating something today

The smileys look up from the plate, calm
A contagious contentment the warm embrace
of a familiar face. In your head you hear
Your mother's voice "potatoes have got
everything you need for life" Carbo-loaded self-care
Reaching for the remote, sprawled across the sofa

A Room Full of Shadows by Praise Osawaru

some mornings you wake to a stamp of silence
in the air, swaying in tune with your heartbeat.

you are paralyzed in your dreams
& you are a breathless wanderer, in reality,

trying to convince yourself that you're not just
occupying space in the world.

you stare into the mirror in your room
& your reflection tells you that you have a condition—

that you suffer from the invisible illness.
maybe that's why your feet leave no prints

or maybe the wind erases them as you go.
you compose an affirmation for yourself

or maybe it's a mantra, you do not know.
it goes: *i am alive! i am not dead! see me, world!*

you say the words over and over again
till your mouth registers the verses.

yet you feel like a ghost hung up in cobwebs
in a room full of shadows.

Things Depression Can't Destroy by Dahlia Garofolo

The three-bean chili in the fridge grows mold
That unpaid utility bill still sits at the kitchen table,
the smudge of spilled honey beneath it crystalized
Poplars still creak and shudder on windy days
People carve their initials into limestone and wood
even after the passionate spark disappears
There will always be sweaty forehead kisses
and little ladies walking patient dogs
There will always be the best day, the worst day
In winter, the sparrows go and leave me to
pick feathers out of my air conditioner
in spring, they scream through my window
Build again

While I'm Battling Depression, I Read of a Man Sentenced to Death for Blasphemy by Timi Sanni

I do not sleep tonight, my eyes choose the certainty of light /
stare up at the ceiling and write poems in the air as the night
brews and boils outside, then again as the night calms in the
anticipation of dawn. The world stops revolving & I'm stuck in
this cocoon, so I constrict my lungs with the need to breathe /
again / to rejuvenate the wilting flowers in the heart of my
being. The internet carries my mind into the horror of a man
who now wears a necklace of thorns. I do not want to imagine
these thorns as skeletal hands squeezing the breath out of a
man, bathing him in his life blood, because can one know
what it means to die / to be dead & still look it in the face,
unflinching? I know so much about sins because their claws
have made a map of scars around my head, but death is an
alien bringing extraterrestrial fears into this alliance of
bodies. My depression is a mirror & blasphemy is a mountain.
But repentance is thunder breaking rocks into powder. I
imagine myself in the body of the judge / in the mind of the
convicted / in the breath of a bystander and find peace in the
remembrance of God and the hereafter's promise of justice
because life is built along the road of death / & death is a
crossroad to glory or another death.

In Patient by H.E. Casson

These metal beds
On either side
Up, up they rise
And here I lie

Tucked in with arms
Crossed in an X

The floor is cold
It cools my back
I count, I track
The seconds tick

I hope I'll soon
Be done with this

The hospital
My second home
I'm home alone
I hum along
(I know this song)
I fall asleep
I'm hidden here

Between these beds

Major Recurrent Depression by Samantha Moya

2:30am, a glass of water straight from the tap,
somewhere between violets and lilies –
(I stopped buying flowers because they were too expensive.)

Kicking off the blanket because it's too hot, pulling it back up
because it's too cold.

I loved your dimples and thought they were kind, and so did
everyone else.

I inherit this disposition; my childhood home is falling apart,
and it's almost funny because it seems like a metaphor but it's
quite literal.
The roof is caving in, the floor is sinking,
and I think the cobwebs have ruined my VHS tapes.

I smashed the clock I remember from my youth.
I wasn't trying to stop time but I was trying to stop something
else from moving.

Everyone says don't take it personally but how is it ever not
personal
Sometimes I read Virginia Woolf's suicide letter to her
husband –
it's unbearably sad but it's also a love letter.

Scars are figurative and very real –
I have the stretch marks from my old body
and the place where I stuck a razor when I was 26.

It's embarrassing how old habits don't die,
you'd think that eventually it should all wash away,

like runoff in the gutter.

In (Your Own Head Nobody Is Your) Mate by Daniel Clark

The bashful day won't dawn. It shirks and skirts
along fleshy walls – you thought all cages must
be metal? that dragons all breathe fire? – tickling
drowned blue orbs. I am inmate and guard, gaoler
and gaoled; sanity means order, direction, structure,
putting every detail in its place like how they sort
elements into that big table then use quadrilateral
voids to paper over the cracks, those pesky vacuums
of knowledge that sink a pursuit nobler than xenon,
argon or krypton… if they can use zips to attach pieces
of cloth, why must I hold myself together?

All the Way Towards Another Tomorrow
by Yuan Changming

Since   yester twilight
Along   the borderline of tonight
With   fits of thirst & hunger
Among   storms of pain
Between   interludes of frenzies or insomnia
Near   despair & desperation
Amidst   the nightmare
At   the depth of darkness
Through   one tiny antlike moment
After   another...
Until   awakening
To   the first ray of dawn

Post Natal by Ellen Uttley

I throw away a mouldy bottle
in a kitchen, filled with crap
piled high with guilt and clutter
bean tins and baby hats.

I walk through my house, in tiny steps
over, and through, debris.
I kick aside a washing pile
that blows through the house like leaves.

From upstairs, I hear crying
and my numbed heart does not tug.
But dread echoes round my aching chest
sucked raw, and dripping blood.

A little face looks up at me,
a new one every time.
Bald and spotted and screaming
and I'm not sure that she's mine.

Anxiety

everything is fragile except this anxiety
by Samantha Duncan

that opens me from the top
by the language's body, where
the blood eclipse we don't talk about
is calendar-event beautiful
(woman hood or hooded woman),
preceding the labor of being read
as bodily and I am everyone's garden,
using the heart reaction
for a petrifying romance
between feet and ground and hum.
love me because you don't have to
and extract the patterns, I'll make
capsules to ingest twice weekly.
take my crescent cycles
to the supermarket with the coupons.
discount my flying spells or
wait until I've boiled and cooled
and crafted the earth to stretch
for us and us-plus and really just me
being able to breathe.
you can love me, you don't have to,
you can close me from the end.

Daydreaming by the Window at Dusk
by Dawn Watts

The better part of the day spent
feeling the weight of an unknown
gloom & doom shadow looming
Around my sleepless body.

It is an illusion, at best;
at worst, just another taste
of the abyss I sink into,
from time to time, just for

the rush of indifference.
There are better ways
to watch the sun chase
the moon across the sky;

however, I have not the inclination
nor the drive to spread the path
with my footsteps mislaid
on a chaotic destination.

My memory is lapsing.
This is not for the hunger
of a new dawn to come
beckoning my undoing.

Gut Reno by Mackenzie Moore

I hope you don't have buyer's remorse
for a house looking pretty good
when you signed the papers
worst case: some flaky grout

Only after months of padding around
learning the sounds of a fixer upper
did you find yourself lingering
on the same creaky board

Jump once
jump twice
you hit the dry rot

You're not going to fire sale
but, if the right buyer
could put money down to fix it,
Well.

Have you seen my finger nails? by
Megan Cannella

I used to sneak
to the bathroom
to hold my fingernails
under cold water.

Water makes things grow.
If trees can grow,
so can my nails.
I stopped biting my nails once
because I was trying to lose weight
because I thought I was in love
because bright nail polish gives me dopamine.

Back Home by Molly-Andrea Ryan

When I float, I float like discarded cotton pulled thin at the
edges and stuffed into ears to keep out the sounds of sirens
on witching hour streets. I float like a jagged piece of coral
split from its reef by crime scene tape, buoyant with rusting
holes. You could shatter me between your thumb and
forefinger. I float like a kite spider drifting across the Atlantic,
my eight legs dancing in search of land, my eight eyes falling
on nothing in particular. I am a car driving the wrong way
down a one-way street. I am a cellophane balloon inside of a
funeral home. I am a wind-up toy tipped over.
Trust me when I tell you: when you hear the sound of
trumpets all in tune, when you see tulips rising from mulch in
shocking rows of yellow and pink, when you feel the perfect
grinding of acorns beneath your feet,
when you walk down the street
and discover each of my multitudes
swaying in exaltation of the here
and now, you'll know
I've found my way
back home.

The Bear in the Restaurant by Emmie Christie

Reda hunched in her chair in the bright, cheery restaurant, her mouth dry, clenching her fists. A bear might as well have been lumbering towards her, the way her chest flip-flopped with nerves. She had no excuse.
Her friends chattered about movies and work while her tongue stuck to the roof of her mouth. Was it the music? The pop rock had a syncopated beat and a predictable riot of chords. It shouldn't have contributed to the fluttering, the aching, the terror underneath her breasts. Was it something stupid like forks clinking on plates?

"You okay?" Seth shot her a sideways smile, the kind that brushed the surface of conversation but never dipped below. He meant well.

"Yeah, yeah," Reda said, and returned the smile. But someone had noticed. She hadn't faked it well enough. Her fingers betrayed her with tremors, echoing the manic quaking of her heart, for which she had no excuse. The bear—that's how she thought of it, giving it some physical form so she could make sense of the senseless fear—shambled closer, and closer. She responded like thunder to lightning; the closer it got, the louder she shook and the more her placid face cracked. What was it? What *was* it? Why was she like this? There. Something whined in the background, a high-pitched squeal. The restaurant's air conditioner.

Something stupid again.
She had no excuse.

"Hey," Seth said. "What do you all say to eating outside? It's a nice day."

"Yeah," Astrid said, on the other side of Reda. The rest of the group agreed, and all rose, shepherding her like a river's current would guide a stick. The high-pitched droning stopped, and Reda swallowed and gasped for breath, and swayed against one of the outside tables.

"This seems like a good spot," Seth said with another sideways smile. He leaned towards her and whispered, "I get it. For me, it's riding in cars."

She swallowed and braced herself against the table. She'd misjudged him. That smile seemed so thin, but it hid a cracked interior.

"Thank you."

Her friends plopped down, and chatted more about movies, and work. Reda listened, and smiled, and even chipped in a little word here and there.

The bear had disappeared.

Slow Healer by Elizabeth Wittenberg

I used to pick at my scabs and point to the scars and say that
I'm a slow healer, rub dirt not for closure, my intention
infection, pity a chance for attention, I would relish in messes
and avoid any lava by piling my pain on the floor, claim calm
came from chaos, what's already broken can't possibly break
anymore -
but now my laundry is folded in drawers, overloaded, and I've
even swept up some dust
living takes maintenance but I meet it with ease, dash of joy
and a sprinkle of trust
I clean cuts and I bandage and I rest and I wait, healing's itchy
and slow for us all
and silently, slowly, self-stitching can start, every scab needn't
become a scar

Morning Portrait by Lauren Peter

                break open my jaw.
constructed without hinges
small bits of self forced to seep
through dry skin
the word membrane.
solidifying aqua molecules
rob the body
of celestial hum.

Rigidity made love to my jaw.
Semi-romantic.
I can't look you in the eyes.

I'm accelerated shyness
soft and unnerved.
I'm agreeing before we've started talking.

My fingers feel three times longer;
I've manufactured more knuckles.

I've stolen months worth of air.

Sometimes, at Work by J. L. Herndon

Anxious, me?
Full-throated performative
laughter, a little loud maybe,
awkward, but the idea just...
just seems so silly
Let me tell it, I'm a leaf
cascading down a lazy river
then basking in the sun
on a sandy bank
At most, a mallard moving
with grace and poise through
the water, working a bit harder
than you might expect
just under the surface

Dopamine by Paris Jessie

I guess my dopamine is shot. What can I do? Before all that I am made of begins to rot. Tonight, I couldn't care less about how long the water runs. Sorry, this is not eco-friendly. It is for the self-tonight. This is where I become something like a painter. Sit and imagine. Doing with a blank canvas. Here in this tub. Yet, I'm still making one with the sun, somehow. I try to feel this water scorch my toes...I'm still waiting. For it to hit, like if the sun were to be lit by its own insides. Something like revival. As if, it will trigger life. Now, am I living? At least for this hot steam, which maybe I am painting as the sun. Like, it is purging something. My body must get extra clean -- I have three kinds of bath soap -- they each are purposeful. So clean that droplets live abundantly upon my skin with no complaints. As a full moon occupying its own clear night sky.

***

I would rather not put water to waste, but a bath wouldn't have held the same space. I would be there resting in things (or trying,) you know, my eyes shower my face. I'm not interested in that. I'm not looking for a space that gives me right back all that I am melting off. I need to cleanse, so that which makes my bones hard and strong can just be. And no, it is not simply a mineral, not for this body.

***

Then, I watch all these things race, race, race down a drain, well, who knows where they go...what they really run into. Not my problem. All I know is that they need to get off of me. If they are to go that far down and be that sucked away it should be an easy, no return, goodbye. As if, it is that simple. Later, I might just dance on the ceiling. Take that.

The Kaleidoscope Says to My Anxiety by Lexi Locket

Unload your thoughts to me
and I will teach you all about reframing.
How a single turn of a memory
can create a whole new picture using all the same colors.
When you freeze with panic sure that your message
will again remain forever unread, I will remind
you to remove the lens of the past
so you can see the blood is not running red,
it is merely the flowers from your new love blooming.
Here, in the present, life is still going.
The tricky thing about the truth
is it can be refracted in so many ways.
The past one of many facets always trying to come into view,
but if you just keep moving I will remind you of what is yet to
be seen.
So used to only reflecting on your fears,
I will bring the present back into focus,
make sure every angle is witnessed,
allowing you to see all the possibilities within them.

Raising Anchor by Cathy Wittmeyer

You thought I fell down the stairs the day
you found me collapsed and screaming
where I stopped on that stone spot in surrender.
My desire to be buried whole
—cold shovels full of slate on my
back and exhaled steam in my lungs—
dissipates with you. You breathe oxygen into my
world like a tree's crown and feed me chlorophyll
to root strong, fill my limbs with windsong.
You anchor me to this ground, Darlings.
If not, I'd be grinding gravel in my teeth
tormented by unpeaceful sleep. You hold
me in fields strewn with aster graced by
grasshopper and honeysuckle borders
lifting monarchs with their scented warmth.
Close my eyes with one hand, take mine
with your other, lead me to these places.
Untether my sandbags and let me rise.

My Body's Tempo by Sher Ting

I didn't mean to interrupt you my mouth moves to its own
body and my body
moves to its own poly-rhythm my teacher at school tells me to
move andante
but we both know the day will rise like a chromatic scale in
allegro and they call me
to my seat but my thoughts are a thousand light-years away
suspended on a coda
spiraling the threads of a perpetuum mobile, a single song in
an infinite-loop motif
playing a parabolic cycle, and I would've asked you to play
Mahler's Symphony No. 2
for the twentieth time that day because he cavorts from
movement to movement
over hours but everyone applauds his form and you tell me
I'm like Vexations, blurting
840 phrases in rapid succession, like it's an impediment and
maybe it is but I'm not a
broken VCR player because I'm not broken and Vexations is
an ironic act of defiance but
there is no irony in my defiance I defy nothing except the
tension of existence
they tell me I should slow down but no one tells the world to
catch up to me they tell me
they wish my feet would stop moving but these hands are
making music,
and one day, maybe, I'll be making symphonies on the world
stage
and I'll strike the perfect cadence in a 5-to-1
and the world will finally clap for me

GERD by Grace Alioke

morning crow escorts the
furnace feasting in your chest with
the rhythm of your heartbeat. what do
you do to the heart losing its crown to the wind?
you crawled as a wounded
snail to the doctor and the banshee scream
that pumped from your mouth
plastered on her table at her report:
Gastroesophageal Reflux Disease.
you're chewing hope as the wheel leads
you to the theatre, and the crumps
grow wings:
I...will... live
I...will... live
I... will...live

Fire by Jonathan Todd

When you get home I'll be sober
on my 5th cup of coffee
out of a hot shower
thinking about the dried out corn stalks
I passed on my way back from the store.
Bought a pack of smokes & chocolate,
chanted worries,
wrote piano music.
Thought and thought,
ceaseless minor notes,
olive oil and kitchen lights,
a single rose as the cooler air slips on.
I decide against lighting the table on fire
slip out for a smoke
still hot from the shower
cells open
a branch wrapped around itself.
Go back and forth
til I remember the last hit of oak
and stare at the cut on my finger
near my wedding ring.
Today I told my therapist I
don't believe in anything.
Not sure what I was trying to get across then.
Still not sure now.

night reading mode by Cynthia Arrieu-King

she gestures toward a pink cloud inside digital forest
wallpaper and says:

    this is my cloud. it contains all my data

uncle moon sees the white screen in my glasses
       and he kicks on night reading mode--
everything white turns black, saves energy, and the print
turns white.
small van icon moving alongside the round white switch
happening inside the diaphanous
the radical / frieze of clouds
a conscience / collective unconscious / collective
it stirs smaller, repeats its circuit ceaselessly
disconnects from variation
disconnects from vary
A polar bear walking backwards through a door repeatedly
gets rid of "I" and moves branches
sighs along the crunch
the ball dropped to the street doesn't bounce
a dead path, footsteps stopped mid-stairs, an immovable
string on a guitar

i'm always going to be sick, aren't i? by Amber Renee

see, there are years of restlessness inside of
my head; history like
    eons of
        nostalgia,
bitter wars,
famine, natural disasters;
enemies building fences between homes
  like separation from god is the true meaning of hell.
// i'm all wrapped up in
this fucking skin; paperthin &
                constricting—
—my body: blood & guts & muscle & bone all   moving
around, shifting bodily fluid.
useless, useless, useless.
there are years of resistance inside of
my head. / i'm sickened by
existence.
/ i want to go to bed.

Roast by Warren Longmire

Every curious eye movement
                is a joist, there is a horse between my legs
        that always moves forward,
        my body is a weapon
        before it is mine.
That is when I learned
            to speak in my father's slur
            of nods, off-center stares, and nervous jokes.
When I started to observe his spasming knee
            watch him watch himself fall again
            and for the rest of his life.
I don't return anything at department stores.
I always look like I know where I'm going and go.
I know the cock of a head dissecting my voice
            detecting the shade of strangle inside my skull.

You Suffer with Me by Rami Obeid

One human body suffering
Two amphetamines to wake up
Three am alarm clock
Four am shower
Five o clock the bus leaves
Six days before the weekend
Seven hours before I can leave
Eight dollar lunch
Nine minutes to wait for it to start
Ten minutes before it's over
Nine times I asked what bus is this
Eight buses at the station
Seven trains at the station
Six ways it can go
Five minutes before my bus leaves
Four minutes stuck in traffic
Three minute walk home
Two benzos to sleep
One human body suffering

Panic Attack in the Umass Yellow Lot by Adam Grabowski

Spring, 2003

Riding the margin
the guardrail sings its sad,
  sad song.
The windshield will not punch back,
hair stuck to the wheel while the blood
  swells in your wrist.
Bald stare in the closing heat,
the blue unmerciful around lines of glass
that shatter spectacularly,
but stay intact.
Another odd fate,
tracing the cut glass that cannot cut you,
nothing can keep the beauty from
  finding your fist—
but what light spills from such things?
There is nothing now save the sweat
  in your throat;
you blink your eyes,
the hazard lights, your heart.

ADHD

Attention Deficit by Gianni Gaudino

The amount of money saved. Scrawling everywhere. Green red, red green. A loose evening, becomes looser, restlessly restless. In the dream, you're running. No, in the dream, you're sitting. The river on your lap. A tortoise is hunted by a rabbit. How many ways can you look without looking? How often can you count, then backwards? Hypochondriac or cursed curious? You've sewn a moon into a blanket. It's never finished. You give it cheeks, a clown nose. You, class clown, sit in the principal's office. He tells you to stop touching his paper clips, the leather chair. You ask *Do you need your bicycle tuned up?* Principal slams his desk, stands to look out his window. In the sky, a cloud shaped like a rabbit drops to the ground. The principal asks *When you grow up, what do you want to be?* Outside, the cloud's breath steams the window. *Put down my stapler, my rubber bands. Are they yours to touch? Can't you just sit there? Can you do that, huh? Sit there and just listen?*

little fishies go swimming in my head by Syl Xing

little fishies little fishies swimming in my head/bite at my nerves and make my eyes go red/ little fishy little fishy nipping at my skull/ the water's sloshing in and out but I'm just waiting for a lull/ little molly little guppy don't eat that card/ just sit and watch all the data crumbling into shards/ film colours blurring bright, spread like poison bitter/ every SIM card I try to catch dissolves like glitter/ little fishy little fishy please make the call/ for now you've eaten my memories and there's nothing left at all!

Self-Medicated ARS Poetica by Jack Strunk-Schwartz

My joy suddenly seizes me with panic and inspiration;
my emotions mix in my mouth.
Uncontrolled, Unfulfilled passions swell under my skin,
threatening to burst out of my chest, and my lungs,
and to peel the nails away from the tips of my toes.

I go for a run in the clothes I'm in,
faux suede boots and a sundress,
just to use my own inertia
to will my skin to stay stapled together
even at its roughest seams.

My heart rattles and twists and bubbles up in my throat with
heat
and a terrible massiveness
I swig desperate lungfuls
of that cool-humid summer sunrise air,
trying to douse those flames of joyous agony
that sear and boil my stomach full of bile and acid and pills.

Autism

Wish by Naoise Gale

I would like to lock the doors to my
Lungs and breathe out all my smoke
In one shadowy breath, I would like
White roses and tramadol to numb
The garroting, I would like to lie
Coffin-ready next to your grave with
My eyes on the sun and nothing
Passing above me, I would like
lanugo and ivy to overrun this
wretched body, I would like to press
my hips into one thin pill, illegal-
white, I would like to hold your
hand and say it is okay, okay, okay:
we are all broken keys.

Joyful Noise by Basil Wright

Boredom is standing in a line outside of an event hall. You and your sibling have planned this outing weeks in advance. The actual event itself will be memorable, even though you know every sound after it will feel like pins and needles on your brain, even though when you exit the building, the sun will be too bright for your sensitive eyes, and even though you'll need to construct a blanket cocoon and nestle yourself into the heart of its warmth, you know it will have been worth it. "No one's getting in here." You will mutter happily to yourself, reciting a cartoon as well-worn and loved as the blankets that surround you.

All of those events are tasks set before your future self. Right now, you are bored. And when you are bored, you cluck. You cluck once, low and soft, testing the mood of the crowd around you. No complaints. You cluck again, louder and with more confidence. As you cluck, your brain sets off joyous sparks of light and color, pushing back the boredom and allowing you to focus better on your surroundings. Your sibling looks at you and you smile encouragingly at them. They're not as much of a fan of making chicken noises as you are, but when you start to clap they join in, keeping you on time to the music you've constructed in your mind. Your sibling shimmies as you jerk your limbs into odd contortions, your soul glowing orange as you clap and cluck.

Others in line stare at your strange behavior, but your focus is captured by the notes whirling within your mind, crafting your bird call piece by piece. Life is simply too short to concern yourself with whether or not being a dancing chicken is appropriate behavior while standing in line.

Farther ahead, a woman turns around to see what the noise is about and your eyes meet. You mimic your sibling's shimmy and continue clapping. You can see the bright glow fill her eyes as she begins clapping as well, bopping her head along to the beat.

To your delight, a few others join you in your clucking: a cacophonous choir of chickens, cheeping and chirping to the same shared song. You take turns clucking back and forth with the man ahead of you, before he succumbs to a fit of giggles.

"This is so weird." He admits, but continues with his bird song.

When at last the doors to the event hall open, an employee pokes their head out to look at the crowd.

"Was it just me, or did I hear a bunch of clapping...and clucking?"

Your sibling looks at you with a good-natured smile and gives one last shimmy.

You throw back your head and belt forth a rooster's cry of affirmation.

Sensory by C.M. Crockford

The clapping hands
(cannon fire)
thousands of them
battering his skull -
sharp sickening shocks -

all the boy can do -

scream.

Mouth gaping
fingers clawing
at temples.

Fifteen years pass.

He hears music in a great city.
He's changed.
He watches.
Listens.

The instruments
build into white noise

inside -
fevered cathedrals.
Delicate wombs.

He knows it is
a tower of sound
where he would live
in Prayer

to beauty.

The violent discord
of this world.

Fragments by Hester Dade

Do not stare. People had been very clear on that, endlessly repeating it. Do not stare. But do make sure to meet people's eyes. Rude to stare, rude to look away.
Sounds congealed in the air around her; screeching metal, bird song, chatter, footsteps, forming a physical mass. Those footsteps came to her, bringing that din with them. Someone stood near and this decision primed itself to pounce. If eyes were a window, the blinds could be shut, curtains drawn.

Something about this person tugged at her attention, eking her thoughts and holding them taut. There was some peculiarity here that she had not identified, a snag in her subconscious, some hidden information.
What people hadn't told her was the optimal duration of gaze wandering, tipped it over the brim from herbivorous curiosity to socially-punishable scrutiny, a mythical period of time that strangers experienced together, a blending of minds, each one yielding slightly before the other, look at my eyes, they spoke a language she could never hear.

The shoes. In the past, no one had been offended by shoe examinations. These were scuffed along the left side more than the right, one of the laces had a double knot, the other beginning to falter.
The lights at the end of the platform changed colour, her train heaved itself around the final turning and into the station. Orange LED lights to take her home.

Sitting down now, avoiding the table seat, facing the direction of travel, she noticed the person had not moved. They half-leant against the fence, hands in pockets, double-knotted shoe tapping on the floor. Finally she could examine their face without retribution.

Their eyes locked with hers. That was all she could remember afterwards; intense brown eyes fringed with long black eyelashes. A physical sensation of gazes slotting together, barbed, impossible to disentangle. Do not stare, for they might stare back.

Revelation by Matthew Feinstein

My memories of you are now reduced to a single night spent
curled up on a recliner while you read me the bible before
bed. I remember how we knelt—shoulders touching, heads
bowed into the void of our palms. Part of me thought you
worried I would rot in hell. Not because I do drugs or have
sex, but because I am different. I still find irony in knowing
you loved me. Sometimes, I make up scenarios you
encountered in the afterlife—discovering heaven wasn't what
you thought or dismissing Christianity before God. Or Maybe
you were right about everything. I hope you explained to Him
why I belong there too. I still don't have friends. At night, I
would hide behind school & watch the boys who bully me
smoke weed & talk about how their Fathers beat them. What I
would give to hug another one of God's children & feel
another body against my own. Do you remember the girl who
lives next door? One morning, we talked at the bus stop &
couldn't stop smiling at each other. She confessed she is also
Autistic. I know you said I'm not supposed to have sex before
marriage, but I want to. How can sin be so tempting? I am still
looking for acceptance. Yesterday, those boys caught me
watching them & they chased me, calling out retarded boy
retarded boy over and over again. I cried out for God. He
didn't answer. I almost let them kill me just to hold you again.
And I'm sorry, Momma, but I can no longer believe in God.
How could I? Four of His children were about to slit my
throat.

OCD

Leaving the Apartment by Jane-Rebecca Cannarella

Leaving the apartment is both a recipe and a spell. Ingredients in a certain order set in threes to unlock the doors that lead to the front stoop. Three cats to find. Three items I need before I go. Three doors to lock and unlock and re-lock in threes to guarantee the cooking incantation of leaving's labor holds. Half-finished spells are spoiled milk and the number of rideshares that have come and gone while I re-work in threes maps the city in miles lost. Inside. Outside. Inside. A magic wand finger swipe to re-order Uber. Re-find the three cats. Hold my face to their faces and tell them I love them three times. My hand on the doorknobs advancing one twist after the other to complete the cooking spell of loss that comes with leaving. At each door, I say the final words to complete the magic meal of going into the world. *It's okay. It's okay. It's okay.*

O see the O Seeds Thee by Omer Wissman

Five is doom three a cure-all
Binging to obesity Charmed
Hate-watching Party of Five
And loving The Wire's S1E5
Where in the dealers' pager code
Five equaled zero and zero five
Coalesced into endless protecting
By numbers my 3 beloved nieces
As in always taking three pills
Of overdosage OCD medication

A Compulsive Soliloquy by Lucy Frost

Because I have no free will, I know I'm going
To chew a strand of barbed wire; I haven't yet,
But I will, and so I have. I haven't felt it yet,
Those metal spines sucking red agony from my
Gums, but I will– and so I already have.

Good at Math by Suzy Eynon

I relay details of the games I've played inside my head since childhood to the therapist who will diagnose me with obsessive-compulsive disorder. I'm seventeen. I assume it's depression, or anxiety though I won't know that term until my twenties when colors appear too bright and the world feels too loud after driving my boyfriend and his entire family over curling roads back from the Grand Canyon. His sister's baby wants to see the squirrels. When we stop at my parents' home, I don't recognize my childhood dog.

I tell the therapist: I pray backwards to outsmart god. *Please let everyone I love die.* I try to think of possible early deaths they might face: house fire, drowning though I live in a desert. If I ask for their safety directly, it might not be granted. I feel guilty for the backwards praying. My thoughts are contagious or can be seen by passersby. I carry a duffel bag on every grocery store or mall run. The duffel bag is as long as I am tall that summer, but I pack it with my favorite dolls and stuffed bears, should the house burn to the ground while I shop for more popsicles from Smitty's.

Older: I count the red letters on the digital alarm clock in long division. 4:24 PM is a good time. An even six. If it's not a neat division, carry the one, map out the answers with an imagined pencil. My days are full of equations though I have trouble passing math in school. *If this, then that.* I envision flashes of terror and flesh for which I have no source document or incident, my brain projecting a highlight reel of tragedy I've never witnessed. I accidently touch my mouth to the arm rest while seated at the circus and, in a panic, ask my mom for a blue Icee. They don't have the red flavor, and blue feels more antiseptic. Blue is the color in which medical instruments swim. I glug it down though I'm not thirsty, and I think I can taste the germs leaving my tongue to scatter so they can be neutralized by my lack of bodily knowledge or by wishful thinking. I close my eyes and trace names and words into the air in cursive without moving a finger.

After the thoughts have a name, my grandmother catches me tapping the inch of white wall just above the hallway cabinet at home as I walk past, a clean space against which to drag my fingertip. I do this to remind myself I'm in the world. I can feel the valleys and bumps in the paint though they are barely visible. "Just tell yourself, *I'm not going to do this anymore*," my grandmother says, though she may be speaking to herself. I nod. I will hold it all inside my head, where I finally understand only I can see.

checking account by Lauren Zazzara

let me check the oven and make sure each burner is turned
off, no I haven't used the oven today but I may have turned it
on in my sleep or perhaps I had a sudden blackout or maybe
the cat managed to turn one on with a precise flick of her little
paw and oh! is that one slightly off-center? *touch-tap-adjust-
push-side-to-side-millimeter-by-millimeter* until it feels
perfectly centered under my fingers but did that just make it
worse and am I subconsciously trying to gas my apartment
and blow up the house and kill all of the lives and living
beings within these walls?

did I put away the hair dryer? stare at the electrical socket
until I can be certain that there is no plug lurking inside and
touch the hair dryer inside the medicine cabinet to ensure it
is no longer hot, *touch-feel*, no it does not burn my hand and
no the plastic box in which the hair dryer is sitting will not
melt and burst into flames, close medicine cabinet door but is
it really shut? can the cat paw it open? and then wrestle at the
shelves until down fall each of the bottles that she can
unscrew to release its poison? Push on the door to ensure it is
perfectly closed but still stare at it for a few seconds on the
way out to make sure

must check the electric kettle, it has an automatic shutoff but
you never know, and I used the toaster hours ago but it may
still be hot, and is the fridge door shut completely or else the
lightbulb inside will get too warm and burst into flames,
touch-push-touch-stare and while I'm at it should probably
check the oven again, are those burners really off?

put on my shoes and then remember I must check the hair
dryer once more as I may have subconsciously plugged it back
in, take off shoes can't drag outside germs onto the floor

where the cat can touch them and then lick her paws and
ingest the lingering cigarette butts or oil spills or pesticides

touch hair dryer once again, it is cool but then must ensure
the medicine door cabinet is once again shut against its
poisons, put shoes back on and lock door but halfway down
the stairs can't remember if I locked the door, and while I'm
checking might as well make sure all the windows are locked
in case a burglar climbs in or a bee zips through a hole in the
screen and I come home to an infestation or an invasion,
which is worse?

but before I do this must take off the shoes again, *touch-push-
touch* all windows shut, shoes back on, *lock-door-unlock-door-
lock-door* several times and twist the knob and push to ensure
it's locked but when I'm halfway down the stairs decide to
check again *twist-push-twist-push*

try to check the time because I know I'm running late but
realize I've forgotten my phone and should probably check
the oven-dryer-cabinet-fridge-kettle-toaster-windows-locks
again once I get inside just to be safe
and decide maybe it's better to never leave at all?

When I was Eight I Learned it was Shameful by Lynn Finger

to be creative & have too much stuff.
My nana beaded blue horses on canvas,
tooled leather & collected fabric.
She was creative & had too much stuff.
When she died, my dad said, "Your grandpa
found tooled leather & collections of fabric
stacked to the ceiling in her room, no lie."
When she died, my dad said, "Your grandpa
found billows & waves of the stuff
stacked to the ceiling in her room, no lie."
Towers of boxes, bed obliterated,
billows & waves of the stuff.
She had OCD & couldn't let go,
kept towers of boxes, bed obliterated.
They shook their heads, gone.
She had OCD, & couldn't let go,
she bled blue horses on canvas.
They shook their heads. I loved her blue horses.
But when I was eight I learned it was shameful.

reminders for an undated morning by Cindy Zhou

if your arm brushes the wall once, you have to go back and tap it twice / those are the rules. i'm not sorry / i didn't make them / it took jesus three days to resurrect / & like him, you live by threes / you don't care for religion, i know. i made you remember / but i'm not sorry / you did this to yourself / you can't blame me for all your problems / so says everyone else, and aren't they always right? / no, they never cared about you / not for a second / they taught you it was right to wage war against your own mind / but maybe the world will be kinder to you / *if you make it to the bathroom before the end of the song* / *if you stack your books at ninety degrees* / *if the droplet on the right reaches the bottom of the window first* / i am only trying to protect you / it's us against the world, don't you see? / i am your most loyal companion / it's what you hate most about me / that i will be here for you always / that i have taken up residence in the scarring on your wrist / that i am not scared of sacrilege, of reverse baptisms / as i force *murder, gore, unchecked rage* into your thoughts and you are helpless to stop it / trust me, i know. i have watched this scene unfold many times / glint of the razor / red sea parting on your arm / you look in, watch yourself drown, & / think yourself healed / if only for a minute.

Eggwhites by Nathan Dennis

My mom says use the hand mixer
Isk isk isk isk isk isk isk isk
But I stiffen my peaks by hand.
Eggwhites, four is a good number
To beat eggwhites in isks of eight,
2 tablespoons powdered sugar
To unfold the proteins of thought
Is six, find two more, bowl and whisk
To make meringues less intrusive:
Whisk count isk four isk isk to eight
To bury eight custardy fears.
Isk repeat return to eight isk
To hold, to eat, to own, to weep…
Isk isk isk isk isk isk isk isk
The meringue weeps. It always weeps.

Everything Becomes Blinding by
Coleman Bomar

A string
Between three falling
Anchors
Is the day unmedicated.
Hours tick deeper
Ticking into night's submergence of stars
Becoming a plastic bag
Around my child head
An utter terror of
Tomorrow's triggered
Sky fall: cement
The busy blood
The clock of walking people
Walking too fast.
I flip the light switch
Eleven times before bed
Every night or else.

Breathe by Marilyn June Janson

Eight AM. Tuesday September 15, 2020. The Center for Disease Control reports a total of 6,537,627 United States cases and 194,092 deaths.

Phoenix, Arizona. Parked at an outdoor mall, I get out of my car, grab a mask from the backseat, and stuff it in my handbag.

A few cars dot the parking lot. I scan the sidewalks for people. None.

No need to put on the mask.

Standing beside concrete fountain, I take 10 second videos of flowers smoldering in the breeze.

I see him in my lens. He is not wearing a mask.

My hands shake and heart thumps.

Deep, slow, breaths. Exhale. A,b,c,d…

Saying the alphabet is my coping strategy.

I toss the cell phone in my bag, grab my mask, and put it on.

Does he have COVID? Is he a carrier?

A sneeze in my direction could spread millions of his microorganisms and infect me.

Run.

Instead, I turn and walk to my car.

Diagnosed as an adult with Obsessive Compulsive and Anxiety Disorders I learned to manage my symptoms.

I pay attention to the signs: sweating, dizziness, and rapid heartbeat. I have retrained myself to breathe.

Relentless worries about health, illness, and dying are my triggers.

Taking prescribed anti-anxiety medication helps to quell these symptoms.

September 5, 2020, Action 6 News Philadelphia reports, "US Surgeon General Dr. Adams advises the states to be ready on November 1, 2020 to distribute a COVID vaccine, just in case."

Pressure from the White House to vaccinate America before the November 3rd elections terrorizes me. It takes years of patient trials for a vaccine to be safe for the public.

Nightmares of government mandated injections plague my dreams.

My peer led mental health support groups stopped meeting in-person months ago.

I have tried Zoom meetings and stopped. I miss the face–to-face contact.

Masks are mandated in town. My friends are going out to restaurants.

Lonely and sad, I want to go out, too.

Sunday September 6, 2020. I leave home At 7 AM for Wal–Mart. There will not be too many people there.

Deep, slow, breaths. Exhale. A,b,c,d,e…

Masks required, I put on two pairs of gloves, and a mask.

Inside I spend time avoiding others and locating items.

I turn away to avoid facing anyone nearby.

Hearing someone sneeze behind me, I cringe.

The store is out of the cleaning products I want. I grab some hand sanitizers and two boxes of gloves.

I pay with a credit card at a kiosk. No need to use a possibly infected stylus to sign my name.

Grabbing my bag, I leave the store, exhausted.

I stop by a park to destress. I get out to stretch my clenched neck, spine, legs, and arms.

Watching a few horseback riders circle the area and boys playing with a Frisbee, this day seems normal.

It is not. COVID has not, "Gone away like a miracle," as President Trump said.

I get into my car, go home, and take a nap.

Breathe.

That Could Have Been Someone Singing
by Jane Marston

Transformative, the mirror shows
a *me* I hardly recognize—an evil twin,
a raging doppelgänger. She-devil's eyes
glow like fired glass. *What's got me so
unstrung? Boom box? Or car door
slammed against the silence
that's my one
safe space?* I run inside;
but the cave still echoes with a world I must
find my way back to, call and response
          spiraling through time
and urging me to follow. It might have been
a dark conspiracy that set these walls
to ringing. Or I might have missed
a pleasant strain. It might
have been someone singing.

OCD Redefined by Bree Bailey

Order. Control. Direction.

I taught high school English for six years.
I state this because I think it is important to know.
I spent six years having my class items moved every. single.
day.

Boards erased mid-sentence.
Papers thrown like thoughts I can't shake into
waste baskets that refused to take them while homework laid
haphazardly on my desk.

Stapler moved to the left
to the right
to the middle.

Mid-conversation my eyes would dart to my class welcome
mat   off-centered   and looking so unwelcome.
How can you feel welcomed if everything is out of order?

For six years, things were always out of order.
I am a vending machine of a person that pleads to be in order.
My mind will never stop fighting for order.
Direction. Control. Order.

Schizophrenia

What fresh horror hinges now? by Betsie Flynn

Admitting the day eyes barely open,
crack-beaming light. My pillow, still damp,
adheres to my cheek, too profane to break
its clinging hold. It's cold, or is it just
the knowledge that waking brings? The chatter
that I can't tear down the stairs to escape
is here and there's no electric, but there's
only eggs for breakfast. Eggs or tepid
coffee that it was too late to drink last
night. It slept alone in the microwave
and I meant to have money today, but
that melted in my palms before I topped
up. My hands are still sticky with it. Should
I climb up the walls and catch flies, eat those?

Schizophrenia by Adedamola Jones Adedayo

elsewhere in the bellybutton of Africa, I approximate as a misnomer
you do not want to measure in litres of normalcy
people say my body is already colonized by an influx of strange audio-visuals
which are toxifying its fractions with syrups of misinformation
& they say my body is festooned with antonyms of realities because
every filament of my thoughts, they think, is naggingly nauseous.
But, I swear, they fail to understand me—
that it is perfectly normal to find heaven inching closer downwards
riding on the mien of regal attachment
& mimicking rapture whenever outside is endearing enough
to see me walk my leisure in abridged sunlight.
they insist that I'm a man with compromised brains,
saying heaven is immobile, a remote delicacy of the surreal.
they do not understand how a cocktail party tenants my room
at the invite of each fortnight when a saturated mind squats
in an emergency suaveness of the wall clock & the standing fan.
I won't tell them about my dead father whose throat is always guesting
at my luncheon table;
I won't tell them since they must be mad not to see the things I see.

i was improving so they told me to by Martina Kontos

tried coming off my pills. we reduced it slowly, five milligrams
at first to see if any of my symptoms would resurface

and they booked me in for an appointment a month later
to check on my progress. i thought i was doing fine

i didn't notice anything particularly wrong except
my stalkers had returned to hunt me, regurgitated

from the depths of the rat-infested city i call home.
they had started watching me in my house again

noting every move i made, every thought i tried
not to think, every curve and angle of my tired

sagging body. but i didn't realise this until i spoke
with my case worker, didn't realise that i had slipped

back into this way of thinking as easily as putting on
my own skin. and so, they increased my medication

again, until my clarity about the clockwork of society
blurred and i felt comforted about everything

and nothing at all because either i am being helped
or my insight is being tampered with for the sake

of a blind world that digs cosy pits for itself to fall into,
pits heated by the warmth of the hell they call obliviousness.

the pills are running out by M L Woldman

doc only gave me enough for 2 weeks
and it's been 1 1/2 weeks and every time I try to cut back
the horror comes like an old friend who's gotten sober
and isn't any fun anymore and wants to tell you
about how great it is to be like him and wane in the moonlight
to the dusted rhythms of Kid Rock anthems
and the horror is also not that
and the horror is also a moldering dinner plate
left in your bedroom for weeks
and the smell encompasses but you can't find it
and the horror is also not that
and the horror is being simultaneously
terrified of and addicted to facebook
and the horror is also the partner
that treats you like shit but the sex is great
so you keep them around
the horror is cigarette burns in the sheets
it is hunger and no hunger it is a crushing humble
it is the feel of bathroom floor tiles on the cheek
it is a human machine shutting down

Beau Black: A Case Study by Alexander Wolff

He watches the shadows crawl along the ceiling.
The hallucinations are worsening, and his prognosis is grim.
The nurses come with his cup of pills each evening.
A month ago, before his mind's unreeling,
he was set to graduate top of his class, but then
he watched the shadows crawl along the ceiling.
The onset was late and abrupt. He began hearing
voices and became delusional, believing he lost a limb,
so the nurses come with his cup of pills each evening.
In patients like him, you can note a blunting of feelings —
psychosis can often cause a man to seem dim.
He watches the shadows crawl along the ceiling.
Remember to note his symptoms after each screening,
so we know whether to increase his dose of Prolixin.
The nurses will come with his cup of pills each evening.
And one more thing before we end our meeting,
don't forget to lock the door to his room again.
He watches the shadows crawl along the ceiling.
The nurses come with his cup of pills each evening.

Bipolar Disorder

When I Wash the Dishes by Lindsey Heatherly

I realize the tides in my brain are shifting
once I'm singing along to my phone
and running the sponge in sudsy circles
inside and around the lip
of the next to the last dirty bowl
that rests atop the kitchen counter
I recognize a calm heart and peaceful breaths
and wonder if my mania is muted
less severe
than the patients seeking care
at the place I am employed
For when I find myself cleaning the kitchen
washing the messes
righting the wrongs
wringing the sadness
for a moment
I find myself happy

If I Cannot Fly, Let Me Sing by Amy Saul-Zerby

It has taken me so long to understand
that I deserve to be touched softly
& longer to learn to lay beneath
your hands without shaking like a leaf.

Most days, I play music constantly
for fear of being alone with my thoughts
that are so often intrusive & always seem
to be out to get me. When I was hospitalized

I smuggled in an iPod & I credit it with my survival.
Because I was raised without a god, I always thought
I couldn't pray, but now I think maybe I've just
never been good at asking for what I need.

When I was little, I was told that if you tell anyone
what you wished for it will never come true.
I learned to hold my breath while passing graveyards
& sidestep the cracks in every sidewalk.

Before my grandparents passed, we sat
for hours listening to their records
& my grandma sang her way
through every household task.

On a good day, I think I'm a morning lark,
keeping myself company the best
way I know how. The next, I am a head case
drowning out my demons in a psych ward.

What a strange thing to believe in a devil

without also believing in a god.
*God: teach me to forgive you for giving me this mind
that I love and hate by turn in equal parts.*

*Give me this day my daily bread & forgive me
my trespasses et cetera I am so fucking
exhausted - please send help – amen*

Manic Train by John Zurn

My manic train of thought and sound
raced down a magic mountain.
Providence bounced up and down,
and signs were pure emotions.
As my train lurched to a stop,
I felt the throttle stall.
When I wrestled with the cops,
they saw no train at all.

let's go to the moon by Audrey Bowers

mania demands. & so we do. she's always so convincing yet
quiet enough to make me feel like she isn't even there. her
ideas become mine, what she wants becomes what i want. in
the end, i have no one to blame but myself.
anyways, on the way to the moon, we listen to pop songs. eat
junk food. cry a little bit. laugh a little bit. *the rest of the
universe doesn't matter*, she tells me. i don't question her.
we get there and the view is incredible . . .
until i realize that mania is no longer with me.
i'm left alone — floating —
amongst stars & craters.

The Tightrope by Aisling Brooke

Growing up, my first association with the term bipolar was when people would carelessly describe the shifting weather. Other associations include hearing people who had changed their mind exclaim, "I am being so bipolar!" or hearing anecdotes of failed relationships, strained friendships, or familial quarrels where people would exclaim the person they were involved with or fighting with was, "being so bipolar!"

I guess these previous word associations are what confused me when I was eighteen, fidgeting in a wooden chair as I sat across from a behavior analyst who was giving me my first formal diagnosis. As the words bipolar floated into my ears I felt confused, relieved, worried, yet hopeful. I was afraid of what that diagnosis meant for me. I was scared knowing that it was something I'd have to navigate and live with for the rest of my life, but I felt elated in having a term to make sense of years of behavioral patterns I never knew how to navigate before.

Despite all of my previous associations and experiences with the stereotypes surrounding this word, I let my diagnosis take a new shape in my mind. For me, manic depression has never been an immediately flipped switch; it's always been more of a balancing act. It's knowing I'm always mentally walking a tightrope between flying and falling. When I'm manic, it all comes a little too easily. It's the impulse, it's the freedom, it's the laughter, it's the recklessness, it's experiencing life on a level that feels like elevated ecstasy.

When the depressive swing hits, it's a different kind of chaotic pull. It swallows the manic me and every version of myself in-between. I feel a lot of shame as my usual lust for life is replaced with exhausted indifference. It's a dance between feeling on top of the world and feeling unworthy of your place in it. It was never a shift in the weather but rather a shift in a tide, where one moment I could easily be floating through life and the next week I'd begin to sink without realizing it until my head was fully underwater. My diagnosis was the first step in not just giving into floating or sinking, it was the first step in teaching myself how to swim.

I'm better now (a rondeau) by Theresa Rodriguez

I'm better now, though I was ill
for many years. Raw memories still
pervade my mind, for I can see,
dictated by insanity,
a fight for every force of will.
Pure manic energy, the thrill,
harsh dangers, foolish acts, until
judgment was gone; but thankfully
I'm better now.
Dark lowness that could bleed and kill,
hard emptiness, death, cold, and chill,
enchained; but now a change in me:
both poles subdued! Miraculously,
due to new pills, (and medical skill),
I'm better now.

spiraling by SG Huerta

i spin my disorder into words, ever present in everything i produce, in every plant i rehome and inevitably kill, in every relationship ended because my extremes were too extreme, every burnt out lightbulb in my small apartment, every acquaintance scared of my highs and every sibling scared of my lows, every picture i paint with too-vibrant colors, haphazard brushstrokes ending up on walls. i used to write that dating while bipolar is like throwing a brick through a window tirelessly over and over i used to write that being bipolar is a life sentence i used to write everyday i write everyday with my disorder.

it never leaves, never ceases to hunger, never leaves never leaves me us it never will.

Dread by Stephen J. Golds

The gut ache that doesn't ease,
the dishes unwashed in the sink,
the laundry murder
shapes on the floor.
Windows left open for the rain.
The fever in the night,
all too black & too bright.
The telephone unrung.
The bills sealed by the front door.
Waiting on tomorrow
like it's the goddamned
firing squad.

Self-Harm

Guillotine Blues by Avra Margariti

I read once that Catherine Howard, Queen of England practiced her imminent execution by placing her head on a chopping block. She was just eighteen years old. It reminded me of how I would practice my own death throughout my childhood: stand on the edges of tall buildings, see how many pills I could fit like marshmallows in my mouth, call it an accident when I cut my fingers on sharp objects.

Years later, I learned that King Charles I wore two heavy, layered shirts during his public beheading. He didn't want to shiver, he said, lest the spectators think he was afraid. I looked down at my arms, the long shirtsleeves hiding all unhealthy practices-turned-habits. I rolled up my sleeves and let the cool air nip at my skin, let myself shiver.

When, by Ron Riekki

when

they took me to the psych ward
the EMTs strapped me in
which was not necessary at all
but they did it because this allowed them

to make fun of me, not exaggerating,
my inability to do anything, because my wrists
were tied—illegal, I believe—
saying, to me, What a waste,

we have real patients to get to, because, I guess,
I was 'only' suicidal, so that makes me a bother for them,
and then when they put me inside, midnight, everyone
sleeping, they put me in a bed that was covered in

piss, how I remember my face hitting the pillow
and the pillow wet, how I got up, told them,
and they told me to get back to my room and I said, but
there's—
and they said, Get back in the goddamn room.

moon reversed by Avi Lentz

the grim reaper's hand spent years gripping my neck and I
was grateful

because death brought me more comfort than being alive.

the prospect used to feel like home but now I understand I
was being choked

trapped in a purgatory where heaven was sticking my head in
a noose and hell was the inevitable aftermath where

my father stumbles across my cold, rotting corpse

hanging from the ceiling fan.

god, I hate visualizing it.

the last time I visited my psychiatrist he said I should be in a
hospital

but I told him that I didn't want to die and was therefore fine

and my mom let out a sigh of relief.

and I'm sorry for being unhappy but it's hard to be anything
else

when your parents passed down their sadness to you along
with the blue eyes

and your body doesn't match your soul.

and I'm sorry for the inconvenience but

maybe I should be in a hospital

and poked and prodded and handled like an animal

like a bomb that's eager to go off.

maybe I would feel at home

surrounded by other kids with tired eyes rather than

a mother who drinks too much and

brothers I can no longer take care of.

maybe I would feel at home

surrounded by bombs.

maybe I would feel at home

surrounded by nothing.

indigo by Yushan C.

Death wears a crown of holly and laurel,
drapes her steed gold and green.

Let me tell you something.

Lately,
She's been haunting my dreams again,
Ebony-haired and regal,
a wraith with a siren's song and elegant wrists.
Now is not your time, she whispers, but gods.
Gods.
I am splitting apart between bone and sinew,
Turning in my self-dug grave in a grove of ash trees.
I splinter like wood,
am set alight by the sun.

Tell me:
Would I get a crown like yours,
if I close my eyes long enough?

When I Was Punished For Trying to Commit Suicide by Nachi Keta

An impulse to end it all, 27 tablets of Amlodipine, and you find yourself in acute medical ward. The doc isn't content with the stomach pump, so he also puts a pipe in your nose, which is not needed- you both know, but he is adamant. "You might die," he says, and winks. You feel like running from here. But one more error and he might put you in a psychiatric ward. So you persist, even though the pipe hurts- lingering inside the esophagus, making you feel you've got tonsillitis. But you can do nothing, except for maybe… pulling it out? Oh, yes – WINK.

When the nurse comes, she finds the pipe lying on the floor and looks at you with a concealed wink. Your throat coughs and then says – "accident."

Wordlessly, she puts the pipe back in and goes out.

An hour later, a man joins you on the other bed with his daughter. *"That devious doc,"* you mutter. *"He is trying to punish me."* "What happened to him?" you ask the nurse. "Accident. Water on the brain. Hydrocephalus," she replies.

The girl appears to be 8. When you ask she says she is 10. You are 20. His father is 30- a bandage over the head and another one over the stomach. A pipe connecting the penis with a plastic bag and another one disappearing into the head- which the girl has to press every ten minutes, else her father will die. But he does not know that he has been operated upon. Water in the brain. He thinks that he is as fit as no one really is. He commands the girl to help him stand so that he can pee.

"Piss in the bag," the girl says, which pisses him off, and he pulls out the bandage from over his stomach.

An open wound. And blood and gore. It is your first time- so bile in your throat. You close your eyes. And then open them. You need to see- you know, that's why the doc sent you here. 10 minutes later, the man's hands are cuffed. The doc doesn't want him to play with his bandages once again. "*He is cruel,*" you mutter. The girl stays awake through the night, as do you, listening to the man's moans. The night is slow. "I'll be more careful the next time," you keep telling yourself.

The Blade by Jerica Taylor

I carry a sword inside me, head to hips.

Some evenings, I want to dance until it clangs against my ribs
loud enough to be heard.

Outside in the sun in the lingering chill of February, light
glints off my chest, blinding. Steel shines just under the skin
of my sternum. Is the blade finally going to rend me in half?
Or is my body exorcising it like a splinter?

I press my hand to this new breastplate. I do not want to die
in the daylight, but I fear turning inward to discover I have
been hollowed, and am still walking.

In an unseen future, something could grow in that cleaned-
out space; a pruned-back bush dormant for a season, a year, a
decade. Any blossom would be an epiphany.

A stem in my hand.

getaway car by Michelle Cadiz

I imagine death like a getaway car,
idling quietly at the bottom
of a pile of pills
a runaway bride, a flight risk, a convict.
on dark nights I picture myself
climbing in – the familiar rush of
relief, each swallow another mile
in the rear-view mirror.
these backpocket suicide dreams knock
around with house keys and spare change,
and I drag them around like a child clings
to a soft toy, up late, unable to sleep.

Bodies without phalanges by Ejiro Elizabeth Edward

I should stop praying to my dead self, find a way to come back
into inhabiting my skin, own my soul like I didn't in the first
act of living. Imagine me floating from the river, from the sky,
into my hair, then my face, then my skin & imagine mother
wearing bright clothes like all expectant mothers do.
                              In death,
there is no such thing as resting forever,
In living
                              we drink to the memories of lost one's
resting forever.
I ache to curve my mother's face into my palms, tell her I am
here but ghosts are what they are,
     bodies without phalanges,
so instead I choose the body of a small child, mother, I am no
longer gunning for my own extinction.

Self-Inflicted by SM Colgan

You have taken a blade to your skin so many times you do not know the number, just that it will be ten years in August on an uncertain date since the first occasion, and is, as you sit, six months since the last.

(It might be less.)

Maybe you should have started counting back at the start, but it is too late now. Too late, except to know that of all the times and there may be 100 with nicks and scratches over those ten years, of them all only one scarred.

6 January 2016, you think. Razor-blade, driven into your left arm in a fit of rage.

The blood made your hands tremble.

(Maybe that was the rage, too.)

A small ridge of scar tissue, invisible to all except you who knows it is there, where to look.

The mark of what you were, once, and may be again.

(You are too old to think it will never happen again.)

Red by Fizza Abbas

it's fun
to use words to paint flowers
when you want to talk about slitting your wrists
it saves you from read koran, talk-to-God kinda advice
who cares why the petals are red
why whorls on my notepad resemble a spindle
onto which a razor-sharp blade could twist -
the euphoria, the joy - your pretty little secret
who would wonder why the anthers look pale
(maybe this is the right shade of yellow)
or why the style looks so weary and tired
(who cares how difficult it is to give birth)
they would look at the flower in its entirety
assuming you're a person: the whole, the self
and you can smile and say, i know i can write well

Eating Disorders

From the Waiting Room of an Eating Disorder Clinic by Julia Beecher

Before we even enter the room, we know each other,
old friends that we pretend we don't notice;
we tap our toes on the floor
cross our arms in front of our chests
and try not to look in each other's eyes.
We see the guilt in our faces
and we hate each other for it,
for our too-big sweatshirts that swallow our rib cages,
the shallow hearts inside struggling to beat
as we fold further into ourselves.
Comparing wrists, ankles, collarbones,
we fall into the hierarchy of beauty,
who is the sickest,
whose skeleton knocks together when she walks,
who passes out on cold linoleum.
And when they call our names one by one,
the last girl to be taken away stays,
sagging in her chair for an extra minute,
hip bones pressing against the hard plastic,
wondering who she'll become in her next life.

Worthy by Michelle Fulkerson

Today I will fuel my body
instead of starve it.
Today I will remind myself that I am,
in fact, more than my anorexia.
Today I will remind myself
what recovery tastes like,
what it smells like.
I will remind myself how far I have come
and what consequences I would endure
if I were to fall down again
upon my throne of bones.
Today I will remind myself what recovery feels like.
I will remind myself that my worth
does not lie in the size of my jeans
nor the number of miles I can run
or calories I can burn.
Recovery is hard work.
It is not all yoga mats and avocados,
not a simple task.
The battle must be won in my mind.
It's effort to live my life
instead of just exist in it.
It's effort to know I mean enough
to stop simply existing.
So today I will be grateful
and know that I am worthy.

ballet class by Gillian Ebersole

I was 13 the first time I remembered the number on the scale. In ballet class, a girl named Marie Elizabeth Marcus bragged she weighed less than 100 pounds, and suddenly the 22 pounds between us felt like an elephant footprint on my chest. I was sitting in the middle of the hallway, stretching my legs into the splits on the part of the floor slanted upward to force my hips into a more elastic position, too afraid to ask Marie Elizabeth if she thought my thighs were big. Somewhere there was a girl dumping the food from her lunch box into the trash can. Every time I felt hungry, I would eat a single almond trying to keep my appetite quiet and my body small. If someone had told me *this is the way to become a ballerina*, I would have stopped eating altogether. Do you remember the first time you ever looked at your body in the mirror? Before I showered, I would stand with my back arched, feeding the illusion of a small waist. The counter in the dressing room was covered in ibuprofen and stray bobby pins. The trash can was full of pre-packed unopened lunches from mothers who thought they were fueling their daughters' rising ballet careers. Years later, my mother took me to a nutritionist because I didn't look good in stripes and I needed to learn portion control. Nobody told me refusing to eat dessert is the quickest way to stop being invited to birthday parties. But this was ballet class, and I had a dream. You cannot possibly understand the distortion of the mirror until you've tried to use your hands to measure your waist and thighs. Say what you want about health – I took a lunch with Oreos out of the trash and ate them all.

First Purge by Anna Wilkes

The girl carries her body as a steed carries a rider,
both unsure of how swift the beast could be when freed from
its burden.
A hillside aches for the memory of her hooves as her spurs
tickle
directions to the uvula.
The hand against her forelock guides sweat-salted skin
towards a gorge. Below, in the quietest space of the chasm,
where the salamanders are transparent
with dark, rests her eye. At noon the air is still.
A cliff is not a cliff when she is the cliff. Above, in the shrill
heat of
atmosphere, in the space where the sun will someday
extinguish itself,
waits her eye. Noon swells to meet the figures and departs
again as shadow.
When an animal senses distance beneath it,
the instincts roil the blood to leap. She leaps, and a long,
high whinny rises from rider, from beast.
Bright sea foam at the lips rusts the bit to the teeth.
The rider tangles in the air with the mount,
and a great heave tosses them together on the ground.
Behind their wild tongues, abyss

Trauma

Beyond the Reach of Tears by Tim Murphy

Sometimes I just want to cry.
And sometimes I just do.
But so often, mere tears falling
are the first rains of the coming
storm, of the crash triggered
by the slightest exertion, even
grieving the life that was
but is no more, the one
I can only touch in dreams
or memory, proves a costly
misstep. One of the few constants –
the tortuous nature of this illness
can never be underestimated.

So today, I draw my curtains early,
place myself beyond the reach
of tears, breathe as gently as I can,
and pray to no one in particular
that it won't be like this forever.

I need more trigger warnings for happy poems than for sad poems by Kika Man

Here is the open grave for all the pleasant poetry I have not
written.
I bury you; you keep jumping on my back.
The nerves in your neck are dark purple, ready to explode.

The moment they do, will you make me drown in your dark
blue blood?
All the ink gushing down my throat, pushing down on my
lungs.
You threw me on my knees, and you demanded to know why.

The soul cannot bear to lose what it has seen.
I know not the joys of writing a love poem, dedicating my
whole self.
Is that why you thread down my spine, pushing it apart, slow
like the silk mouth of a coffin.

I hurt you but not so you could puncture holes in my stomach,
closing them with nightshade. You are the most beautiful,
fulfilling thrill of feathers.
Gallows of letters spelled flawlessly. The moon to guide my
ship.

To suffer by the hands of the incapability to plead happy
is to be burned paralyzed. To be torn apart with a pair of
tweezers.
I dream to embrace you, though it may shred us into ashes.

at beach, fisherman's son by Martins Deep

"Water is for drowning"
the fisherman's son tells me,
as he goes picking clams
into his leaking pockets.

"The sea gets thirsty, she calls
you by your favourite wine"

Whispering in my ears,
he says, "Ask for driftwood
whenever you feel the ears
of your god open to your lips"

We return to his shack,
by the beach, and find his kinsmen
embalming a body.

"He died last night" they say.

I look behind me at the wet sand
seeing only my footprints.
only my footprints.

I am Here by Anastasia DiFonzo

Because I didn't die.
Because one month ago,

I stood at the edge of a bridge
and didn't jump.

Because I continue.
Stay is a verb, like the *tumble*

of leaves to the bottom
of the canyon into which

I didn't fall. Once,
at a job interview, I was asked

what kind of tree I would be.
Eucalyptus was my answer,

because it's my favorite.
Imagine now thinking

I am what I love.
I am almost there.

Ice Burial by Lucy Zhang

Let snow bury old Xu Fu Ji crispy peanut candies & half-digested rice. Sugar is better sent into earth than left to grow mold in a plastic bag. They tried to send me away, you know, like snow can hide footprints as much as it allows them to exist. Pretend you don't see them: shadows, imprints, like Bigfoot marched through. Life might creep under crystals, absorbing syrup, desiccated coconut, refined colza oil, *building breathing growing* until their sky melts. Find me frozen, snappy limbs like silver fish bones, before I make it over, where problems are fixed just because we bury gold with wrappers—an unmarried scarecrow meant for mending, an inheritance of jewels wasted. I am not grass, unintentionally weeded yet without casualties. If only I could be like that, puncturing ice even before spring, instead I am strung like old wires on the zither, though they sounded beautiful once, still taut against the wood board hammered, glued, sanded in the basement, left there to play a dirge of silence, for daddy long legs & mice & bones to pirouette. The candies flake & crumble, but I rattle against bars waiting for rain to either flush away snow or freeze over. I didn't eat them, the ground did, swallowed like a supernova—is the hope, transgressions forever hidden, so I can stay.

Electroconvulsive Therapy Made Me Forget Many Things But Not Grief by Ashley Sapp

It's quiet when you forget. At first.
They warn you that the stimulation will result
in memory loss, but they don't tell you that
what you'll be left with is grief.
You will trade your recollection for your mind.
You will face a gaping hole where experience used to be.
There is sadness in forgetting, but you'll regain yourself, too.
Pain fades and scars emerge.
It is slow but not gentle -- unfortunately.
There is a price for everything. This, too.
That is why there is grief - you are better
and yet you cannot remember how or why.
It is quiet when you forget because
the silence is what remains. After.
The silence is a sorrow sonnet, reminding you not of what
was lost
but instead of the fact that you lost it.
Say hello, though, now.
Introductions are my new saviors,
tiny initiations of person, place, and thing. Petrified and
preserving,
I am returning. It is not so quiet.

a renaming by Shitta Faruq Adémólá

for Ernest

i pluck a flower this night, and ride an ass to a city.
the birds meet us at a seaside and sing, burn elegies
into the tiny spaces in my ears.
the night's colour is dark. i want to pluck a moon for
a lamp, tell the stars to lead me to that place where my
father sleeps; i want to go there and cry, cry and dry my
tears on his grave.
a ghost does not shake in its tomb when prayers enter it,
so, i pour the moon into the body of his grave,
and tell him to sleep well. *sleep well, father.*

What Scales Are For by Jo Matsaeff

In one of its editorials, *The National Geographic* explains
that pangolins are too naïve for this world and that it
makes them the most poached species ever.
Their only self-defense mechanism being to curl up
into a ball and hope for the best.
But what they don't know is their own armor
is what will have them killed in the end.
Their scales are worth millions.
I take a look at the funny-looking creature
and this little guy looks right back at me before
slowly walking to the next page of the magazine,
unaware of the gunmen who might be reading right now.
Just like him, my ancestors had to adapt to survive
a world that didn't want them, passed on their scales to me
hoping I'd be the first generation to make it.
And I hope they're not
watching right now thinking
it wasn't enough.

Roaches by Kristin Ryan

Its clawed hands scrape along the inside of my skull until all I can hear is jagged humming. It doesn't matter that I have a book coming out, a husband who loves me, or that I haven't purged in eight years. When the humming becomes unbearable, I calmly tell my husband I want to die over breakfast.
***

I watch from the ceiling. Two lovers sobbing, one restraining the other on the floor. *Dirty, dirty, I'm dirty,* the woman howls as she tries to claw at her arms, tries to lunge toward the bathroom to rid herself of what she cannot name.
***

In the backyard, he pressed my five-year-old spine up against the fence. I felt cool air for the first time. Dead grass clung to my dress. Wasps hummed in my ears. My bare feet burned when I ran from the house, the lie propelling me forward.
***

Children often mistake hands for roaches and other bugs when recalling memories, Bree gently tells me in her office.
***

I wanted to pretend it / was a dream, but / every morning I choke / on weeds. // Choke on sunlight / and fences, the / hum of wasps / splinters in my back. // The bathroom, / where the nightlight flickered. / The tub full of soap scum and dirt. // A shadow, more cool air, / roach in my underwear. / I start peeing behind bookshelves, / avoid bathrooms, / take short showers. // For a decade, I purge behind dumpsters, / in cars, and fields / until there's blood, until there's bone.
***

Think of it more as resting. You're sick, and you need to rest a while, the psychiatrist says.
The nurse passes out used crayons, explains how coloring is a coping skill we can use once we're released instead of killing ourselves.

In the den, I change clothes behind the couch, *hurry up, hurry up* nightgown over leggings; *he can't see me* the sound of cartoons crashing in the background.

While I was crying in her office, Bree said: *most predators have cartoons on to distract children. Most likely he was trying to groom you.*

No, no. I should have been smarter. I should have *known.*
You were a child. It wasn't your fault. It wasn't.

I'm given Risperdal, the kind that melts slowly under the tongue. I wrap myself in a thin, white blanket. I stare at my reflection in the glass, fighting sleep. Later, the nurse finds me covered in sweat, thrashing as she stands over my bed. *You kept shouting stop.*

By morning, I sit on my bed and weep, too afraid to move. My parents come to visit. They don't know why I'm crying, or why I'm here. My husband comes to visit. I tell him the thoughts and memories keep getting worse, and I don't know what to do. He takes my hand and cries.

I dug a hole that drank my grief by Tyler Puffpaff

when my mother died I developed a burning desire to garden
as if I needed to splice myself with the Earth to survive

and if I'm being honest I was already familiar with the
temporary relief physical exhaustion allows—

I just wish it were enough. this became my religion:
gouging the Earth with each vehement spade

jolting the muscles that held her hand all day,
shouldered her worries when lifted into her chair,

and this chest that tendrilled its support through the winter.
I try to cement the grief down with my heel

as if I could expel it out of me and into the ground with
enough harrowing.
but it comes back. I am stubborn. I repeat.

still, I replenish so much feeling so fast
even without a shovel I am always digging.

                    I have so much to give.

somewhere, a hole is drinking my grief to the pulp.
can a soul really contain this much?

it never stops;
an infinite hum. lulling. distended

They Made Me by Maria Picone

go to the darkened room to perform my trauma,
no warning, threatening to expel me if I refused.

feel small, a tiny mote of protest swirling in a vast
maelstrom, arms bound by this mandatory evaluation.

risk my scholarship on a one-afternoon "fitness" test
a run without screaming, a gauntlet without swords

present myself red eyes bound hands to the bored
professional who took one look, said "You're probably fine."

This is not a big deal.

pull my bones from the wash cycle, proclaiming
I was normal, *then* I was not. Okay.

Names Have Been Changed by Susan Triemert

Shot, Shot, Shot, Joe chants when his college roommate walks in.

My boyfriend Joe bought his first house, and we are ready to celebrate. Within the hour, a plastic cup of red wine spills, and bleeds its way deathly close to a white rug. His twin brother stacks a pyramid of empty Budweiser cans inside the garter snake's cage. After I slam a few Screwdrivers, the party becomes a blur of broken lamps and hearts, tear-induced laughter, and drunk girls cackling down in the basement. Just before 3:00 a.m., I hear mating calls from the spare bedroom and spot a guy snuggling up to a decorative pillow in the bathtub.

Joe and I fall into bed, and my head spins on the pillow. I wake to grey and plaid shadows, the sheen of a wrist watch. I hear the tinny sound of a mattress coil before I see what looks like Kirk, Joe's friend from his bartending days, toppling off the foot of the bed. I recall images of Kirk--seconds earlier--trying to jam his hand down the front of my half-zipped pants. I rub my eyes as I try to make sense of it all. I had been lying next to my boyfriend, had felt safe enough to feel the electric heat of his body, to inhale his dank, boozy breath.

I rattle Joe awake, and he tumbles back to sleep. I tiptoe into the next room. Kirk appears to be asleep in the LazyBoy, with his mouth hanging open--he looks like a baby turkey vulture. I stare at his half-open mouth, imagine drool dripping from his hungry upper lip. I want to shake him, turn on the lights, wake the whole damn house, ask: Why, Why, Why?

149

I stop. *Have I dreamt this whole thing?* A side effect of my antidepressants is that they heighten the sexuality in my dreams.

I slip back into the bedroom, shake my boyfriend harder this time. I insist that he go and check. I tell him that Kirk is faking, that he's not asleep. Joe moans and sighs as he is ripped awake, as I tell him what happened, about the thud on the carpeting. A water cup knocks to the ground, an overhead light buzzes on, the mattress bows as he scooches out. I follow Joe to the next room, still wondering if I'd been dreaming--I did increase my dose of meds. Kirk is no longer in the chair. Joe walks to the front door. Soft flurries had collected on the mounds of hard, stubborn snow. He checks for footprints in the fresh flakes--reports there hadn't been any. No freshly grooved tire tracks either.

Later that day, Joe calls. How could you be so sure? he says. Your drugs make you crazy.

I bite my lip. Know he is done listening.

Before hanging up, he adds, I'd never be friends with someone who would do something like that.

I imagine going to my psychiatrist later in the week, to inquire about the drug's side effects. Was it possible, I'd ask, that I'd imagined it all?

Flinch as the doctor grazes his hand over an exposed knee, across a sleeveless shoulder, and tells me it's all in my head.

Seks by Bella Aase

baby blue buick
carpeted seats
wide squealing hinged doors
it wasn't traumatic
just confusing
another ten minutes of play
between catch and swingset and making
living room towns of matchbox cars
and cardboard boxes
real worlds to a five-year-old
wearing blue's clue's tank top
and frilly shorts and velcro strap sandals
hairband holding bleach blonde strands
mom says keep the computer room door open
she calls my uncle a raypest
but i've never met him
my cousin eli is the best playmate
six months older but not much taller
dirt stained basketball shorts and baseball jersey
shared love for grandma's mac n cheese
he knows new games besides barbies
and dress up and we have the most laughter
outside in the yard and driveway
all of a sudden he climbs into buick
and tells me to follow close the door we
get close together and he bumps his hip on
mine over and over and grunts like when
he throws a football across the yard
what are you doing?
we're having seks
what is seks?
it's what grown ups do
we're playing grown ups

Broken by Abu Ibrahim

They'll tell you to go, and you'd grudgingly accept. Maybe after hurting the ones closest to you, maybe after breaking your lover's heart—you stare into their eyes and a monster reflects, maybe after realizing healing has nothing to do with the prescriptions. Tepidly, you admit you are bad for your own company. Sometimes, you can't see you're falling apart because you've been veiled by denial. Living is injurious; the world wounds us in ways we are blind to. At the temple for broken people, you sit in a ring trying to complete the circle of healing. First, they say their name, before calling out their demons. One after the other, there is an outpouring of ache. Being vulnerable is a pill, and you doubt if you have the stomach for this. The shrink nods in your direction, and you realize for the first time, to heal, is to be honest with your wounds.

8:05 am by C. Cimmone

I chewed up two of your Norco for breakfast

9:16 am The dirt daubers were busy twitching their abdomens in the garden, hauling away tiny bits of mud I'll never do anything with, so I smoked the rest of your weed you had in a socket.

11:25 am I got carried away thinking about what to do with all of your t-shirts until I smelled the skillet burning bacon grease.

3:45 pm I used all of my Xanax up; I dug around in the medicine cabinet and gobbled up your leftovers, too.

10:57 pm I forgot to lock the front door, so I laid there on your side of the bed, hoping an armed stranger would burst in and save me from thinking anymore about you being gone.

sick little girls by Kristin Garth

"We've got a sick little girl - we're just trying to take care of
her." Jamie Spears

"My client has informed me that she is **afraid of her father**,"
Sam Ingram, attorney for Britney Spears

My father threw chairs, said prayers, beat me
until I begged, hands wandering between my legs,
controlled each penny I received, worried
only how he was perceived — not by the dregs
at public school — by saints upturned lips
would fool, also my Laura Ashley dress,
too snug against my breasts — can't help but glimpse
the way they shudder as the lungs suppress
the shrieks of a violent distress of
the sickest little girls, minors they can hide
away from the world, legally, even call love,
with padded rooms and rubber gloves, statewide
commitment takes two relatives to sign.
Threat I'll outgrow though Britney remains confined.

you shaped me for sacrifice by Isabel J. Wallace

I exist in three places. In the first, I'm nine and digging a little grave for the first rattlesnake I killed. I bury it in two parts: body and shovel-separated head. I hate myself, but the dog doesn't die. In the second, I'm four and being dragged past the rabbit hutch. There's one less. I can't count them but I know, I know, I know that there will be rabbit blood on blue sheets. In the third, I'm twenty-four, sitting on a park bench, and thinking about being nine and being four. I'm thinking about how I was taught to buy protection with pieces of me. If I lied about the abuse, he wouldn't kill a rabbit. If I swallowed any feeling for the rattlesnake, I could protect the dog. They said the rattlesnake cost less, but it wasn't the rattlesnake's fault (wasn't mine—). Saving the rabbits cost all of me, but I never shook the conditioning ("you're saving them, a little hero"). I was a price. I was a price and I paid my price. I paid it without understanding the worth, the lie.

Grass and gravel crunch beneath my shoes. I'm twenty-four and saying, "No surprise I'm fucking broke."

Translating My Worries Into Something More Palatable by Charlotte Akello

Mother asks if I can go and stay with my uncle,

I know widows swallow responsibilities that their husbands died from and sometimes their eyes hold death/but they know they are the only hope;

I want to tell her no/I want to tell her guys are not being trusted/that sometimes blood becomes the thing that takes life from you

I crawl out of my skin and put my thoughts into words (in my notebook that stays under my bed)

What's the world without a mother/how not to show a man that you love him/how do we cut blood ties/how to deal with men who come in the night/synonym for uncle/how to kill a man who touches you in places mother warned you about/ how to fake my own death or make it real.

I don't want to go...

Trail by Gina Tron

A man, common, an everyman
asks me as I walk on a deserted trail
during a global pandemic
if I wanted to go to
the most secluded spot of the mountain top
to put my mouth on something that his mouth has touched

I never wander up the hill again
he probably wouldn't have raped me
but that's a mountain of a probably
maybe, more like it
I'm scared of getting raped again
but I could handle the rape
I can dissociate from that
I cannot handle
being disappointed by the people I love, again
because I love them
and would like to continue doing so.

smile baby, smile by Shelby Bevins-Sullivan

forgive me–
   i don't mean to disturb you,
the thunder in my head rattles every night,

your eyes, a somber shade of lapis,
whimper, *isn't my love enough?*
   and it is, it is, it's always enough–

i just forget that when a hand
   lands firmly on my shoulder,
it's your pink, plump, sugared lips

awaiting our wake-up kiss,
     not the thin grin of a breathing gargoyle,
     the one that clawed my breasts,
     tore my labia til they bled.

being still helps me get through the hours,
     you say, they all say:
     smile, baby, smile,
     smilebabysmile,
     ssss mmmm iiii llll eeee

but smiling is what got me
hurt in the first place.

dusk is a purple heart by Lamont B. Steptoe

from blueness
above blueness
crossing
jagged foam
to verdant green
tropical water world
where the wind
is a bloody cloth
where songs are sung
by machine guns
where songs are sung
by machine guns
where sun and moon
are ambushed
where dusk
is a purple heart
and Buddha is thrown
from helicopters
uttering haikus...